SWEET YOUTH

There is a crossing on that stair, a place of ease,
exchange of breath, quiet passing, kiss and cease.

ALLEN GROSSMAN
SWEET YOUTH

POEMS BY A YOUNG MAN AND AN OLD MAN
OLD AND NEW 1953 - 2001

A CONVERSATION ON THE STAIRS ABOUT
LOVE AND KNOWLEDGE

A NEW DIRECTIONS BOOK

BIBLIOGRAPHICAL NOTE AND ACKNOWLEDGMENTS
The uncollected poems in this volume from the middle of the last century were printed, most of them, in three books: *A Harlot's Hire*, Walker-de-Berry, Inc., Cambridge, Massachusetts, 1961; *The Recluse*, Pym-Randall Press, 1965; *And the Dew Lay All Night Upon My Branch*, Aleph Press, Lexington, Massachusetts, 1973.—A.G.

Book design by Sylvia Frezzolini Severance
Manufactured in the United States of America
New Directions Books are printed on acid-free paper.
First published as New Directions Paperbook 947 in 2002
Published simultaneously in Canada by Penguin Books Canada Limited

Library of Congress Cataloging-in-Publication Data

Grossman, Allen R., 1932–
    Sweet youth: poems by a young man and an old man, old and new, 1953–2001 / Allen Grossman.
        p. cm.
    "A Conversation on the Stairs about Love and Knowledge."
    ISBN 0-8112-1522-9 (pbk.: alk. paper)
    I. Title.
    PS3557.R67 S84 2002
    811'.54—dc21
                                            2002008595

New Directions Books are published for James Laughlin
by New Directions Publishing Corporation,
80 Eighth Avenue, New York, NY 10011

CONTENTS

Foreword to *Sweet Youth*   xi

PART ONE: *tira tira tiralou*

Blue   3
The Room   5
Where Are the Objects of Desire?   6
Clear Light   7
Does the Moon Move or Do the Clouds?   9
The Ballad of the Bone Boat   10
Monika's "You Enchanted Class"   12
A Curse   13
Lilith   14
Bang!   15

PART TWO: *study the school*

Face East, Song Bird   19
The Sands of Paran   20
The Pilgrim   22
Berlin 1955   23
Storm Coming   25
Tales of Odysseus   26
Louis, the Middle Man, Says Something   28
The Cry   30
Endymion   31
Rose of Sharon   33

PART THREE: *the knitter*

The Knitter   37
Not to Die Now   38
The Unfinished Man   39
Flick   41
Rivers   42
The Breaking of the Law   44
Spring   45
Womb and Tomb   46
Lyra   47
In My Observatory Withdrawn   49
Jew at Calvary   50
Monika's Lars   51

PART FOUR: *salutation*

A Loving Salutation   55
Reading Late   56
The Recluse   57
Blameless Physician   61
The Baptist   63
The Final Girlfriend of the Western World Is Light   64
Getting the Child to Bed   65
Voyage   66
Coming Upon the Azores   67
Masked and Veiled   69

PART FIVE: *blaze*

Total Eclipse   73
Blaze   74
Words   75
The Turning Tree   78
The Murderer   79

The Death of Beatrice   80
The Wreck   81
The Ghost   82
Sweet Bird, Sing   83

PART SIX: *the house sparrow*

Come into My Garden   87
The Order of Life   89
Husband and Wife   90
House Sparrow   91
Amesbury   93
A Tree of Two Seasons   95
Spring Song   97
Chicago   98
Pompeii   99
The Incomplete Life   100

PART SEVEN: *among the dead at troy*

Among the Dead at Troy   103
Moving the Trees Around   105
Everywhere I Find the Jews Killing the Imagination   107
Beersheba 1973   109
Sail Simplifies   110
Fons Bandusia   112
As for the Towers   113
The Thrush Returns from the Waste and Void   118

FOREWORD TO SWEET YOUTH

READER! What is made begins with the unmade. This book contains poems by a young man, the SWEET YOUTH of the title, written and published nearly fifty years ago, and contains also poems written in this last year (2001) by the same man old. In this book an OLD MAN, and the same man young, meet and acknowledge one another for the first time and pass as on a stair—one going up and the other down.

The story of this book is that encounter—*that* passing—in which is expressed all the capacity of each of them for love. The action of that love is a kiss. In that kiss, as these poems say, is the whole cultural process (from unmade to made, from made to unmade) by which, from others, living and dead, we become makers, bound to give back to the world's store whatever it may happen we can do. That is the interest of the love story and that compels the inevitability of the school.

◆

One benefit of living out a long life is that you can see, introspectively, this process (this procession) of cultural regeneration in your own life and can show it to others in theirs. That's what a poet does, or any conscious person to whom it is given to *consider* and then speak. A book of poems (both for the poet and the reader) is what a life looks like when you stare at it, as it were, over your shoulder backward, and think about what you see as a succession of moments (poems, performances in the theater of mind) out of which a "life" is made. Each poem, each profound moment, begins before speaking, departs from that boundless speechless origin (primordial), and ends up after speaking at the *outer limit* (all too close to the eye) of knowability of final consequences ("history") which the lesser story, these several moments one at a time, compose—a story expressive of such coherence, and only such, *as can be claimed* when you "stare back" and then think about what you see. This book is composed to articulate one version of that lesser story.

✦

The poems of the SWEET YOUTH are printed in Roman letters (formal, upright, unashamed). The poems of the OLD MAN are printed in *italic* letters (in motion, leaning to the right, as if against a wind). The two speakers, young and old, in their difference, are important to one another. That importance arises *in the relation across difference*. They pass on the stairs, as I have said. But which one is going up and which one is going down?

✦

When the poet, anyone who thinks, sets out to write (when anyone who intends to make anything sets out to make that thing which he or she intends), *this universal, conscious maker* (you, reader, or me) enters the world's workshop and looks about. *There lies, ready to hand, materials, the lumber out of which whatever we make must be made.* What is made begins with the unmade, or (what is the same thing) the already made by another in the immemorial history of making always going on without knowable beginning or end. The unmade is the warrant of freedom with its hope, and also of subjection with its horror. And this very self (unmade by us) which we each of us are shows through all our making (our loving, our acknowledging, all our composing) and is the interest, the concern, the meaning and the reason for, and therefore the authority of, all our making. At last the unmade is the death of the maker—because the artifact only endures subject to the laws of its materials.

✦

Both the SWEET YOUTH and the OLD MAN think about death. But death means something very different for the SWEET YOUTH, on the one hand, and the OLD MAN, on the other. The SWEET YOUTH remembers the death of not having been and then coming to be—the Seven Days of Creation. The OLD MAN knows too much about the lumber from which his frame was cut. His death-thought is of having been and now soon ceasing to be. It is the inevitability of this strange sameness and difference that makes the early poems and the latest poems, the first and last findings of any aware mind, kindred and necessary one to the other, because explanatory one of the other.

◆

The confidence in the world which this book of poems, *Sweet Youth*, intends to speak to you of, as we pass on the stair—intends *to hand all the way over to you, the reader*—is not a TRUTH, but that other kind of knowledge than truth, poetic knowledge, which people have in common because we, all of us, are bodies for sure and are aware. The body is the stable ground of all reference, the principle of our common knowledge, like the difference between right and left hand, fundamentally logical and poetic.

What the old man knows, and the young man does not, is what the young man will write. What the young man knows that the old man cannnot remember (it is as if he never knew it) is the unwritteness of the self. Both are wise but neither knows, and that is why they desire one another. Love in this book is desire for knowledge of the other one.

When I read out poems I have made, or prepare my poems to be read silently by others, I become aware, as I have said, that all making (everything that anyone can call "my making") begins with the unmade and ends in the unmade. Any making, such as poems, but also thoughts, judgments, actions, building, greeting, all speaking and the rest, any thing that I or you make, begins with the unmade, the poetless, and intends to add to the store and presence to mind, of the unmade—intends to add, not to the honor of the self that makes, but to the honor of the world the self has not made, the world of other persons, of institutions, peoples, gods and concepts, and also the trees and flowers, the beauty, the boredom, and the horror. Making begins with the unmade and intends to return its making to the unmade (the beginning of freedom with its hope, and subjection with its horror). And this self, "unmade" by us, of which and for which we are composed, shows through all our making (our loving, acknowledging, our composing) and is the interest, the concern, the meaning of, certainly the authority of, this maker and, at last, the death of this maker—as the artifact only endures subject to the laws of its materials.

Everything in the here and the now, for the SWEET YOUTH and OLD MAN, has changed in time—words, voice, world—in that sense they are totally historical—except this habit of making poems, i.e., speaking with the expectation of being overheard by you. Tell me, READER, which one, as between these two, knows better? Is experience an enlightenment, or a darkening?

AN INVITATION

Sweet Youth, let us revisit the mountain meadows
by moonlight. Something is coming to pass.

Old Man, dilectissime, *take this kiss.*
Death is the slightest deepening of life's solitude.

Sweet Youth, dilectissime meus, *kiss me again.*
Kisses are the only worth, as the poet says.

✦

Old Man, here begins snow, the former snow,
vanished except for this—and the latter snow.

Sweet Youth, you are the first and the last student,
the inevitable, the only one given to my hand.

Old Man, snow upon snow, snow upon snow,
snow upon snow. Until your death and my death.

✦

Sweet Youth, reading again is the last blessing,
revisiting the meadow in the moonlight.

Old Man, let us give the meadow a name.
YOU say what name we shall give the meadow.

Sweet Youth, this is the meadow called "consideration"
or maybe this meadow is called "hand in hand."

✦

Old Man, what does consideration see
by moonlight, what constellations?

Sweet Youth, the pole star is gone,
the ever fixed.

Old Man, we have no way. Sit down with me
in the dark, where beasts have lain.

PART ONE

tira tira tiralou

BLUE

Florence of Arabia, I will marry you to Andrei,
the boy bell-founder. From far off comes his song:
BONG, BONG, BONG. On the day he marries you,
his song will change to: tira tira tiralou.

Midwinter. The cold house grows colder.
I hear the garden owl announcing snow
and departure. I didn't understand before.
NOW the owl-sentence is clear (who would've thought?):

Anybody can marry anybody. But
somebody must say some words, like these:
FREEDOM, IMMORTALITY, GOD.
(It's practical good sense, dilectissima,

cheap housing for married people). Without
FREEDOM (BONG!) winter cold stops the heart.
With or without IMMORTALITY (BONG!) you die;
but without Immortality you die in terror.

As for GOD (BONG!) look in any face: the flash
is painted with our likeness. —From the tower
in the next town, over our winter fields,
the note of the boy's great bell mounts up,

heavy with information: the great code.
The wind stops for the slightest moment,
a bird in flight stumbling at the indiscernible
threshold of a bigger winter, as if

in that very slight turning of breath
an immemorial covenant was again sub-
scribed: FREEDOM, IMMORTALITY, GOD.
Nothing new. But the bell's soundings

are different: BONG. BONG. BLUE.
Can you hear it, dilectissima? *No longer*
one and then one. Now two together sing:
tira, tira, tiralou. I MARRY YOU.

THE ROOM

A man is sitting in a room made quiet by him.
Outside, the August wind is turning the leaves of its book.
The door is open, everything is disclosed, each leaf, all the voices.

The man is resting from the making of the quiet in which he sits.
The floor is swept, his books are laid aside open, his eyes are open.
All the leaves and voices are outside in the restless wind.

Soon he will rise, or take up a book, or someone will enter;
Or, perhaps, a leaf will come across the threshold, or a voice
Will blunder through the room, blind and unanswerable on its way
elsewhere.

But now the room is quiet as the man has made it.
Everything in its place is at rest inside the room.
And the man is at rest, seeing each leaf, and hearing all the voices.

Where are the objects of desire?
The sheath, the cradle, urn and chalice
Of my sword, my infancy, my ashes and my wine?
O I am knit up by loneliness—
Sharpened, purified
Beyond the imponderable decision to love
Or to believe.
Everything that I am not flees from me.
This is not solitude peopled by phantoms,
Imagined things to which some good adheres,
But rather critical vacancy
In which desire wells as from a sourceless fountain
And spills itself into a cloudy basin.
Living in my desire I feel the anxiety
Of endless fall.
Where are the objects of desire?
The sheath, the cradle, urn and chalice
Of my sword, my infancy, my ashes, and my wine?

CLEAR LIGHT

"Look! You're going to die," they said.
I looked hard, and I saw nothing.

Everything I love comes from you to me.

"Up on the roof you should be able to see."
In the end birds gather in spectacular numbers.

Everything I love comes from you to me.

Some man might think it out, if he went on thinking.
I might think it out if I went on thinking.

Everything I love comes from you to me.

We have gone astray like sheep. We do not hear
The reed pipe conversing to the hills.

Everything I love comes from you to me.

The reed pipe conversing and the hills' reply
"In a clear light nothing is lost."

Everything I love comes from you to me.

In the air where the small birds are
"In a clear light, nothing is lost."

Everything I love comes from you to me.

In earth where the mute stones are at home
"In a clear light, nothing is lost."

Everything I love comes from you to me.

"Nothing is lost, nothing is lost."
The streams reply, "Nothing is lost."

Everything I love comes from you to me.

"Where in the starlight is my friend?"
"In the next bay, laughing and singing."

Everything I love comes from you to me.

"Nothing is lost, nothing is lost."
The song we sing, "Nothing is lost."

Everything I love comes from you to me.

Sweet Youth! Return once more. Once more I come
with something in my hands. —Remember your question,

"Does the moon move and do the clouds stand still,
Or do the clouds flee across the moon's face

quick as wind?" Sweet Youth! Return and listen to
my final dream, my dream of answering:

—A lounger now on the high white cliffs, of
chalk and flint composed, an Old Man, his scattering

hands folded on his knee, gazes at the sea
in storm, and at a sinking wreck and all the lost

that in her are. Night falls. Silvery moon. Now
night wind drives black clouds across the moon's face.

The man rises. Affection descends the long stair in tears,
with nothing in hand. But, mounting up, here comes,

on the same stair a Sweet Youth with a studious look,
honey-colored hair, and a miraculous book.

And there is a crossing on that stair, a place of ease,
exchange of breath, quiet passing, kiss and cease.

Then all continues as before, under the moon,
sometimes black, sometimes bright, always alone.

I dreamed I sailed alone
In a long boat, a white bone.
Like a strong thought, or a right name
The sail had no seam.

The mast, and its shadow on the sea,
Fled like one high lonely tree
Bent with the weight of the wind-fruit sown
By the cold storm.

It was a dream of dignity
When I steered on that plated sea
With a seamless sail, and a boat like a bone,
In a fair time of the moon.

There was no rudder in the long bone boat,
The compass was a stone—
The air was empty of the deep-sea gull,
And gone was the cry of the loon.

The sea and the sky were one dark thing,
The eye and the hand as cold.
Unbound was my hair, unbound was my dress;
Nothing beckoned or called

But the words of a song
That had death in its tune
And death in its changes and close—
A song which I sang in the eye of the moon,
And a secret name that I chose.

And this was the song: "Straight is the way,
When the compass is a stone

And the sail has no seam, and the boat is a bone,
And the mast is bent like a tree that bears
The wind-fruit of the moon."

And now I sing, O come with me,
And be at last alone,
For straight is the way in the dream of the boat
That is a long white bone.

MONIKA'S "YOU ENCHANTED CLASS"

Going from you makes me sad.
We had a colossal adventure.

But now
In your heads wild flames flicker
In your hearts distant birdsong,
gorgeous rumors.

Not today but in a new time

you, wild Bengal,
will become a gentle FATHER ANGEL.
You, smart girl,
will insist with your fist
at a strange table.

A CURSE

In my youth
        I studied
                the *impossibilia*
Setting a tree of language
                in void space
                        on fire
—Like a dark lake
        consumed
                by the hot winds of heaven
Or the bed of the same dark lake
                seething
                        with dry bright grass
Which the lightning
        ignites.
                But now
The ax
        is laid to the root
                of all the trees.
From not knowing
        there follows
                a certain gratitude
As from not willing
        there follows
                a certain distracted haste.
But the barren tree
        the sanguine fire
                will consume forever.

LILITH

I was the first made woman. I first wept
Alone in the changed light of evening in a chamber
For love.
I am in the trees when the wind visits them
With altering voices
As the year clothes and unclothes.
Non est Bonum . . . it is not good
To be alone.

I rose with the maples on the evening of the first day
Flaming.
Of all birds I loved the Tanager for his scarlet.
I would have filled all the spaces of his song,
Enfolded him as the orange flame enfolds
The blue of its own cooling heart.
I cannot say what I could not have been:
The plenitude
Meted to his emptiness,
The heat of which he dreams in the cold night,
And the light
All lost.

Oh Tanager, first and last you are a slave to shadows.

Each tree sings,
The leafed tree with the fullest sound.
I am Lilith, the unmarried,
Whom three strong angels could not haul
Back to Eden.
Let Adam howl like a whipped child
The loss was my loss.

I kneel upon the bank, and take my hair down
Weeping like a woman.
Let exiles and altarless men worship me
As night without stars.
I spread my hair over them.

BANG!

(at the garden window)

BANG. This happened before. What IS IT?
Terror-at-heart. A bird-corpse broken
has broken in! On its blind road elsewhere,
this dove did not see me. Am I nothing?

O dilectissima mea, *CAN'T you*
imagine another life? You have ways.
We did talk sweetly, so long, about such
great affairs. GOLDEN MEXICOS.

—No longer! Nothing more to be given.
No great store unclaimed. Not anything
heaped up, among leaves. On this time-road,
a broken bird, inside my heart, lies dead.

✦

With a strong hand and outstretched arm
holiness desolates earth (JERUSALEM!).
The birds flee blindly every way.
Plainly, plainly, I am nothing.

As it was THEN, it is still. Louis and Beatrice
return, in their lighted, illegal cruiser,
announced by fifty cannon, salvo after salvo
and Bang! Another broken fugitive.

—But I notice how, this summer, there is
(this is the DIFFICULT, the hard to understand,
O dilectissima mea, *beauty's question)*
much birdsong in the garden st st twitter.

PART TWO

study the school

Face east, song bird.
Study the school—:

"To think is to die."
On that art you can rest

the whole weight
of
night and day.

Where the sun burns,
there is
the infinite of interpretation.

To your left is north,
to your right is south,

under your tail shadowy
west.

I have questioned them all, Miriam, Aaron
And many who hated him more, of what he saw
Those days and nights of storm. In the plain
Fear compounded deity of desire
And memory, for to a querulous people
To be leaderless is an Egyptian servitude
And they were wanderers in a hard place.
But *there*,
Beyond the consolation even of shrubbery
Under a sky complicated by light
Some novelty was endured that I would like to know.
My mind is in the wilderness with Moses.
Here beyond Pisgah, where he did not come,
Now Joshua is dead, I cannot think but
Of the sands of Paran. His brother is a priest.
Miriam remembers the leprosy he gave her
For carping at his arrogance of insight
And the woman of Ethiopia in his tent
Who was his wife, and knew him face to face.
They can no longer say where he is buried.

I seek the wilderness again, and light
Falling in flights of arrows; the long
Way round, and the imminence of the mountain where
The ploughshare does not serve as an adequate weapon.
I would recover, not the dream,
But the confrontation, not the nice complement
Of olive and cedar, but the complex face
That talked with Moses there, and spoke on stone.

I am not the remnant, and I lack even
The hatred of my people. Yet in some dawn,

Usurping the hierarchies of the birds,
When I have climbed up there to where he stood
I shall in my own voice speak of my need.

Cambridge, 1953

And did the swan sing "Kristallnacht"
Sitting upon his freezing lake?
   Oh yes, I heard him as I passed
And blessed him for his song's sweet sake.

   And as I passed I lifted up
I lifted up my heart and eyes,
   As someone wandering with a cup
Feels the fountain rise.

   And are those echoes ringing still?
And are these circles echoes of that song?
   As one stone sleeps beneath the mill
The other grinds the corn.

   And as I passed I saw the names
Like burning babes upon the air
   And worshiped them, a pilgrim cold,
And called them everything that's fair.

   O Muse, the ox has set his foot
Upon the flower and the root.
   The ox that turns the mill has trod
Down the vestiges of God.

Under Penelope's restless hands lay down
Gypsies and Jews in an agony so remote
I cannot remember. We were a web of wanderers,
Undone in a room, and resolved into like threads.

Muse of agonies, you who were the witness,
This is your voice. Yet haven't I learned here
Something about ruins? The choir is gone.
The rose is blasted out, and stares. Coloring
The air the four evangelists hang in the apse.
Who was here to say, "Let those who have failed
Be stripped naked"? All the gold of the church
Is turned out to the night. Time,
Mute intimate of agonies, hide me
From the suffering that from that choir
Issued out. Who were they that were not spared
Even their flesh? I can hear the bells striking
In the blackened tower. Memory has forgotten their hour.
Where the rose was, I can see stars.
They are departing.
The world lies all about me in its indetermination:
This is truly nakedness, when the bones are so well known.

A streetcar grinds around the church,
As if it were not there. There are no trees.
They cut them down with kitchen knives the cold
Winter of the liberation. Among the stones that made
The walls assemble the confraternities of the maimed;
And here and there a man or woman
Will ascend the welter of the ruin of the familiar
Seeking, like sound bricks, what still is.
They built heavy, in this country, elegant cathedrals.
Children knelt here. And in the last battles

Which are always on the most familiar ground,
The devil's private army died here. Tangled
In ivy, new bells are rising in the city.
Hedges are remembered. But on this ground
Life will no longer serve the living in the place
Of innocence. Memory is a candle
In a crematorial oven on an eternal All Souls' Day.

A tall woman picks her way among
Rotten stones
Who has minded the cooking pot the ten years
It has had no mistress, and handled other
Common things, the flesh rake and the iron litter.
She has seen the grave of unknown thousands
Touched with one inadequate wreath, and has not
Stooped to add another flower.

                              These were
Not her people, but the murderer had kindred things
About him, like women and a fear of dying.
He will rise again. But we
Are no longer so many as we were

To be destroyed, and have not happiness enough
To be among the victors after any battle.
The young have died too long before the old,
Who cannot answer so intense a glance.

STORM COMING

I am an old man (70 yrs in Jan.)
who has stepped
from the road into the field. Storm,
coming from the southeast,
brings thunder. Then early darkness.
4 PM, July 16, 2001.
Something is going to happen.
Soon light will require a champion.

Who?
(Darkness covers all, and an untimely owl.)

But the champion of light lies dead
under a stone
by the turning tree
where the plowman rested.
There are imaginary voices
everywhere
on earth and in the air
and one real voice, Song of Songs.

It says: LOVE IS AS STRONG AS DEATH
(but no stronger).

The hallucination of good weather
Can deceive the young. Others
It maddens, when hair becomes
A crop of crocuses and terrible forsythia
Forks from fragile fingers. To be dead
Is easy and passes into habit.
But to live
Surpasses understanding. The outraged
Senses mourn when flesh unfolds
Like an unreachable conception
Suddenly achieved.

Wrapped in a stinking skin I lay all night,
Rehearsing lies, until at dawn he crawled out
Blinking the bright windows of his eyes,
Foul, impotent, sinewy, and old.
I gripped him savagely, and he became
Bright water flowing to the sea;
Then a cold serpent, then a flowering tree.
At last he was a glorious woman. With a knife
I came upon the order of my life.

Conceive a coast shuddering and sublime,
And then a ship utterly cast away,
Its people poured like pollen on the waters—
Think then of rocks gigantic
And the unwatered deserts of the deep they guard,
And marvel how I came ashore
(Being neither wholly god nor wholly man)
My knotted beard wrapped round me like the veil
That Ino gave to one who could not love Calypso
Wholly beautiful. And know from this

That in the infinite patience of Poseidon
All our impatient imaginings
Are sealed at last,
As by an unimagined consummation.

Death is dreamless. Let me die.
I am too old to dream. Who cries
In the night on my hard bed?
It is I
And is not I. I cannot cry.
I have paid my blood with blood
All the days of my life,
And now my blood demands my soul.
Who will weep for me?
What lawyerly tongue will make my terms with terror?
Old men have many enemies.

Beware of your male children—
In the least familiar places,
In your dreams, they hunt you.
They steal life from your love,
And then conspire with time to steal your life;
And when you're old they come in dreams,
Sweet children weeping tears,
And steal your sleep with questioning.

Begot in rage, and married with a curse
I have struck life from death
Like fire from two struck stones. Subsiding
Into age as in dark water
I cannot say what I have done.
A dead man hurled me into life.
Each blow he gave me marred my son.
We stand—
One dead, one dying, one yet to die—
All still as stone.

Less words these words than memories of pain:
Cursed be my sons, as I was cursed—
Let love breed its assassin
Generation after generation
Until the spark ignites no more
And the green world sleeps beneath the sky
Untormented by fire.

I who have never dreamed dream now.
Each hurt I ever had or gave
Has got a voice.
I am a child hunted by children;
Sleep is no sanctuary, and the familiar silence
Bred in the soul by violence
Turns to clamor at the hour of death.
Sweet children whom my curse has turned to stone,
This is your father's soul.
Hounded by your weeping I grow cold.
Rooted within the eyes of the old
A pale cataract spreads its flower.

THE CRY

Sleepwalking, having it both ways and none,
Doing and undoing the raveled sleeve of care
With fluttering fingers, getting nothing done,
Blind with streaming hair,
You nursed our child and put it down
Hours ago. Something else that weeps
Drives you up the hallway in your sleep,
A lost thing, sister to the thing you lost.

To me you are a ghost with bared white breasts
Fainting with hunger for a thing you bore
But, being dead, can never reach
Although you wander in an ecstasy of care
Making of my bed a haunted wood,
A wound, a grave, something not understood.

To fight the crocodile you must be young.
Grown old you accept your mutilation, and wander
Into the swamps to fight the greater monster.
Whatever your skill or luck you always die,
But no one will have seen you slip headless
Beneath the mantle that floats and flowers on the water.
At seventeen the nerves of your seamed body
Are strung like the strings of a lute or a strong bow.
When the crowd has gathered
And while the pitchman describes your past escapes
As victories,
You stare into the pit until the water clears.
You arouse one beast after another with a stick
Until you find one big enough to kill you,
And drag it out by the tail, already weary
In your arms and thighs of this vast scorpion
Which neither wakes nor sleeps. It would escape
Back to the time mirroring water of the pool
But you distract it, and display it to the crowd,
Knowing that the beast has summoned you, and commanded you,
And is your destiny.
Then like a lover you cover it with your body.
You link your arm beneath the staggering clawed
Fin, and lift it over on its back.
It is as white as moonlight.
                    Now leap back.
Now it is most dangerous although it swoons.

How like Endymion you are in love with death.
The crowd awaits your reapproach,
Half-naked, to the panting creature
Which they each create, and in the instant
Cower from, crying to you, "Have mercy, deliver us, or we die."

Now you go forth to tempt the beast which never
Can be tempted, and not for the love of mercy
But for the unacknowledged love of death
Drag open the great rake of the jaws,
And breathe your breath into the ivory maw.
Your muscles quiver, and your skin is white with terror.
—But it is stayed, and we are still upon the shore.
The crocodile crawls back into the pool.
You pass your hat along the concrete wall
Which guards the pit indifferent and dreamless.

Come into my garden. This August is the last.
This night, the last summer night.

This hour, the last hour of the night before sunrise.
I think of you, day and night. Dilectissima,

come into my garden before the sun. Take my hand
in the dark. . . . "How cold the air!"

"How cold you are." The first step down is
a high step. Sublime breath

swells and subsides in the garden among leaves,
each one an emerald sentence

spoken by the oak in the dark. In its mysterious well,
the oak stands sentinel.

—Here is a path. It is for considering.
Look left. Consider, in this dark:

"Tiger Lily."
Look right. Consider:

"Bleeding Heart." Listen!
Someone comes.

It is parent
dawn.

She: "Look at the path!" He: "What do you see?"
She: "The path is strewn with letters."

"Dilectissima, *out of these letters I can form no word.*"
"*Allen, out of these letters no word can be formed.*"

He: "The night has fled away. Look again."
She: "My dear, look there! That is Rose of Sharon."

PART THREE

the knitter

THE KNITTER

"Bring me a book about how to die,
not sentimental, dry as sand.
—A book about nothing."

Bodies remember. The pain in her
phantom limb is a memory,
a page
about nothing.

"The time of death can, sometimes,
be chosen.
Death cannot be chosen."

Among the watchers, one of us knits
(click, click, click, click, click), one needle (the right one)
visible,
the other (the left one)
covered.

"Even
a blind person is permitted to
consecrate the new moon."

At the last she sent away all the watchers,
also the knitter
who said:
"Not a scarf, nothing finished for use,
a trial piece, to see how it is done."

—Her last word:
"Hermetic."

Not to die now but sometime after this,
In a larger room, elsewhere, in fresher air,
Some place favored in memory, perhaps a hill

Among the bleaching bones of sheep, hawk-killed,
With the cuckoo's muted horn in ear,
A pleasure boat below reaching for open sea—

A moment when the wind rises or falls.
But not as I now am, wearied out upon
The fool's errand I have sent myself.

The fleeing forests of the mystic winter
Cast shadows on my children at their play.
This April is as cold as summer's end;
It is like a young man's mind or like a girl's
Wasting passion on the thought of death.
I had hoped for greater certitude than this
Hard sentence written in the spring:
The kabbalist is not a married man
Nor is he rabbi who has forked himself
In children. The God of the created world
Is April's hostage as am I. Therefore,
Let us begin our meditation on
This evil and uncertain weather.

Like birds out of a solitary Oak
My children rose, who now in April's evening
With sweet unsettled cries return to rest.
We are shards of one majestic being
Which dreams of its own beauty in the spring,
As of recurrent shapes the sea
Is never satisfied. Love shattered us
And shook us into such separate beings,
As now the spring discloses by its cold,
Wandering here, as once, God did at evening
Searching for his own image in the garden.
Regard this Oak, late flowering and latest
To lay down its leaves, God's tree, despising change.

The world is stern, unfigured, without description,
Containing no mystery or treasure.
In it labor is lost, and love
Cast out like wings upon the water without resting place.
My plow prepares the winds and my great horses

Labor in the empty fields where no tree
Shades the turning. The seed falls,
And falls, through sight and thought and dream
And darkness more profound than dream,
And falling is its fate and fertile rising,
Blossom and decay, harvest and hoarding.
This heart, this plow, and this my ponderous team
Prepare the desert of the world without repose.

—There is that in me which will make time
Remember my incompetence
And how it was that to these ends and images
I offered up desire, and did persist
In thought and wore the darkest garment in this
And other seasons, and did not greet the spring
With condescension to occasional reality
But rather did prolong the meditation
Of one thought
Until, in my purity, I had become
Perfectly accompanied, or perfectly alone—
This is the sacrament of resolution.

Let's go to the movies and hold hands.
The lights dim. The stars
come out.
And then the skyline of Granada
is visible,
from every seat the same.
This is the theater of mind.

He: "I've seen this one."
She: "But not with me."

At that moment a distant bell is heard
to waver and vary because the wind
has stopped
and then begins again
—as a man
who suddenly remembers he is dying
rises alone, and turns to
leave, deliberately,
before the end.

Outside, loitering children whisper,
"Here come the real people."

RIVERS

I

As rivers turn to ice and stop their flow
And still move on in the dim place below,
So I have learned to hate you and grow cold
And yet my love flows to you as of old.

II

I am a wilderness of springs and fountains
Yearning for the maiden who draws the water
Or for Narcissus with his looks of love,
Preferring rather to be deceived than unvisited.
Why do not lovers, weary of the quest,
Weary of the image also? Why still desire
What they no longer have the power to pursue,
Or still pursue what they have known entirely,
Or still trust that which has betrayed them?
Weary even of sleep, I am not weary of you.

III

Time with the beloved is a road
Without her is a labyrinth
In which the clue is a question—
Does the body's solitude and the soul's
Await the same comforter, or will there be
Three when I at last lie down, and will they be
Living or dead, my delights,
And what can these thoughts mean?

IV

Inconnue de la Seine, moth empress,
Dire feathered head, and withal sweet.
If even for the lovely joy is hard,
How then shall I, being much less beautiful,
Become less strange? God-visited
Are women who are beautiful,
And therefore wild for easier beds
Where bloom not amaranth but lilies.
Inconnue de la Seine, you are very beautiful.
Your mouth is not like Nietzsche's blotted mouth—
Why do I find you chronicled with the dead?

V

I do not understand nature in solitude—
Nor how it too flourishes alone and in the dark;
In the summer world I burn and it glows, both of us
In the same dark, together and unaccompanied.

Were I less solitary I then would understand
For desire and ignorance are one passion. What presence
Assuages the great tree and the empty-hearted river
When in the wind the one cries out, as the other always flows?

Strapped to the bed of circumcision lies
My son. This mutilation ties
You to the fathers. They will never let
You forget, or your flesh be enfranchised ever,
Though you pray all your life long.
They set you early on the rack, infect you with a fever
Of remembering. In the marriage bed,
When you are naked, there the sign is red.
There is neither meeting nor mating but the past
Cries that you've been waited for and wed already—
I will not bless this mark upon your body.
For you the hurricane is rising fast;
I feel the horns of Moses in my head
And Law wrenched again from the dead
Hand of deity, and I descend out of the blast to you
Mad with loneliness upon this bed.
But I reserve also the rage
That broke the Law upon you like a rain of stone
That other time I saw you so could yearn.
The Law is broken, baby. I will not ascend again.

SPRING

The fields are rotting as the ice lets go.
The barking water fowl are now come down.
Still is the river water, still and brown.
The water is not white, though it was snow.

What will breed and what will come to be
Out of this flux and rot and brutal cries in air?
Can the cold hearted animal take thought and stare
Into the unremitting springs of history?

The strange desire not to love again
Or, what is less strange, to offer up desire
To the great god of war who once knew Love,
Compels this utterance while the rain
Burns like fire along the wall.
The Lord is my shepherd, and I his animal.

Same pit: birth pit, ash pit.
Pry them apart if you can.
Do that. It takes two. More.

The life of the poet is
the story which the poem
by the poet tells. That

is all the poet has to
say. The story is always
the same and different.

Could it be otherwise?
No. It never is otherwise.
Always the same, it insists,

insists on difference.
Always different womb and
tomb and therefore bound

to the labor of approach,
the untrue, the insistent
I am you, true and not

true, even if thrown I lie
dead silent or wide awake
screaming in the same pit:

how the body bears particular
weight, how the eye reads
in that particular light,

how death is seen the same
from that window, at that
hour of the day or the night.

Everything is water, and the moon moves it;
The stars move nothing, but are not unmoved.

Out of my love for you
I wish you to be moved as stars are;
They are in heaven, and ever deeper in heaven
Are hurling backward their reddening light.
We go by sea, and pale as we wander,
And not the moon only, but the wind also dismays.

Not only stars becoming blood, but blue stars too are in heaven.
Beyond the moon it is intolerably bright,
Still and quick,
Moving of old, moving forever. In Lyra is a ring
Lit by a star blue as the sky. Think of it!
Motion which is not flight or departure,
Which seeks not hopelessly to meet anyone,
Unmeaning, unquestioning, free.

The eye of the wind is passionate; who can go into it?
Now it is autumn, the fall of the leaf.
We do not know which is the first falling,
But the oak is the last, if it survive the lightning.
We will not die, we will be buried under snow
Where the wind stares
And the moon draws the restless waters over us.
Heaven is not earth, but the earth is in heaven
Where man was not created nor ever will be
And all is unsown and unharvested
And ever will be.

Under the drifting snow we drift
Down, down, down. But up there

All moves with no mover—perpetual tearless departure.
But not alone or together,
Unsheltered and untorn, unawaited and unmourned,
Not whole and not riven,
Moves for no reason, or for a forgotten reason,
Not knowing we know it moves.

IN MY OBSERVATORY WITHDRAWN

To whatever face
Real or passionately imagined I turn up my eyes,
It is the Beloved who hears among her stars.

When I lay at my mother's breast
And took delight and gave delight
It was the Beloved who nourished and upheld.

When I took off my shoes, and with the forgotten stealth
Of a hunter searched the peaks of the mountains
Where only night and the storm-cloud darken the stone
It was She who put on the mask of sternness
And the tongue of steel and turned toward me the tremendous mystery.

And when I lay face upon the face of all my yearning
And body in the womb joyful, She stood close behind the veil,
Never until then so close.

Now in my observatory withdrawn
I am given up to the sky, and strain my eyes across the spaces between.
On cloudy nights I sit in a lower room dreaming,
And listening to the tick of the heart, until the wind rises
And the clouds turn and turn and depart, and I climb
To the unroofed upper room once more, and adjust my instrument
Praising the wind.

I have heard trumpets until I'm deaf,
And swept the floor, and awaited dancers
To beat the resin into the wood.
I have understood the word,
Forsaken, who have never understood.

Should a star fall, it would be
An unripe fruit out of night's tree.
I will greet it—and say *just this*:
Until I have no time for you
Because I'm madly in love, until

Tortoise is outrun by hare
Up Golgotha because the dove
Is flaming and inflating its throat,
Until the ripening of the stars
Hurry, hurry up. Death will not wait.

MONIKA'S LARS

Then there is
LARS.

LARS is one dog
who knows
how to save
a little girl.

Do YOU know
how it must
be done?

You're right!

He jumps into the air
(in a friendly way)
with the little girl
on his back.
He doesn't even
bend his knees.

(Anyway, dogs don't
have knees.)

Then he turns right around
and flies backward
gently

dog-angel-wise.

PART FOUR

salutation

A LOVING SALUTATION

On a silent, crepuscular, and August
afternoon, when it rains, games go on anyway.
But when rain is accompanied by lightning,
and thunder follows lightning on the count,
the field empties. Then, a voice out of the night
is heard by all, offering loving salutation
to the one Jew by other Jews cast out,
because he owneth no other minister than thought,

who dwells in a wet bush and writes long letters
about the exploits and sufferings of light
and sends them to the nations to make it known

that thunder offers to the seed of Abraham,
by a scattering hand, wherever strewn,
tremendous syllables of greeting.

Mumbling my office and thinking about my boy,
Anxious and half asleep over my book,
While dying oak leaves plummet down and stop,
From the great garden oak in the still air,

I find myself uncommonly awake
Upon that passage where the warrior shelters
Under the sacred tree which is his father's,
Sarpedon wounded, Zeus's child and care.

And wonder how the god did shade his boy,
Not being everywhere but only *there*,
That tree, that natural thought, quite unexpected
The father's mind being unnatural,
Easing the pain that time, which did one day
Devour the child and leave the god in tears.

THE RECLUSE

I

My life is bountiful, although I dwell
Absurdly in it. I am a bird disgracing
This most lovely tree by my poor plumage,
Half grown and badly worn as if unowned.
About me grow such gorgeous blossoms
I have long since called them eyes of God.
On this white tree amid blue flowers of air
I am the only thing improbable.
To my own senses I am all unreal.
This bright world lacing and unlacing
Cannot create me in another sense
But stares out of its luminous blue eyes
Unwondering at my wind-eaten wings.

II

I live beside a stream that does not flow,
And I have grown as still as my profound
And household river. I am as cold as ice
And do not know how light inhabits me
Making my heart a crystal cave, untenanted
By anything but glory. I do know well
That, underneath, the sea searches the stream
And claims it, beyond its power to contain
Its meanings, or withhold its tearless well
From ocean's fields, resalted by the rock
The name of which is always Niobe.
And by this sign I know that I shall love
Again, and thereby grow both swift and dark.

III

My house is older than my life and therefore
A continual instruction. Through it

Pours the song of birds as if it were
Not there. I read in Ovid at my table
How men were changed from being men
To something less deceivable, and I
Am changed by solitude until the light
Lives through me and my body is no more
A breeder of shadow. On darker days
The rain inhabits me, dim without sorrow
And chill without love. From my reverie
Woodpeckers wake me with their stony bills
Searching in the rotten walls for food.

IV

In especial I am haunted by Apollo
Who loved Daphne, Daphne who became
A tree. I follow her across the fields
Crying, "I am the god of wisdom offering
Knowledge of the past and of the present
And of what from the dark source beyond us
Is yet to flow." And I too see her run
With the dark certitude of a natural thing
Knowing this is not love, whatever
Love may be, that at her back cries out
I am a god. Her father was a river
In the vale of Tempe who changed her
Into laurel which is forever green.

V

Something has nested in the chimney
And makes a phantom fire with the roaring
Of its wings, stirring the ashes on the stone
In the act of comforting. I warm myself
At night beside this fire, and listen to
The song in the nest that floats above me like
The sea that lives and does not live in shells.
And who will tell me that I do not pray

(Being unfashionable) with the profoundest right
Of a deserted man to that vague thing
Which has usurped my empty hearth and altar
And is a common bird, and yet unknown
To me except by cries, and by the breath of wings.

VI

Wild iris, the hidden violet, and clover
And a dozen jewels nameless to me
Rise in the rank pasture by the river.
What is more real? And these too evening
Encompasses, and night devours altogether.
Fireflies remember the nightly death
Of flowers, luring the wanderer by the river
Tranced in the fire of memory and the dew
To consecrate himself to quest for those
Ten thousand grails. I am not the knight
Of flowers. I am the beast rather
Seen by Gahereth drinking of the river
From whose belly issued the cry of dogs.

VII

Much can be said in dispraise of memory
And I deny it all. I shall not live
In this place long—the meditation
On the signs and sacred images of desire
Must have an end. This place I shall revisit
On the shrunken stream in autumn coming up
The current in an old tin boat to where
My house untenanted is hid by fainting blooms
Suffered by summer to grow much too long.
And I will greet the god of the place
With temperate rejoicing and call him by his name
And for the dance
The hamadryads will forsake their trees.

VIII

What is this wind which twists all,
Letting nothing be final or blooming,
But all, at once, rooted and wandering?
Is this the hour and the minute of the end,
When the gigantic oak goes straying on the land
And streams withdraw to caverns underground?
Far inland I behold the driven gull
Afloat upon the frothing crests of trees
As on the uninhabitable sea.
And I am paralyzed with loneliness
And cannot think except to cry aloud
Holds the wide world any slim and glittering thing
For which my heart's need has not a use and gratefulness.

BLAMELESS PHYSICIAN
(in memory of Thomas French)

Your parakeet abandoned you among
The trees of Colorado where it died.
St. Francis had better luck with birds.
I am grieved
More on your behalf than on my own
That I am dying out of reach
Blameless old man
Who could teach neither boys nor birds.
Such love as I can bring to mind
I now declare to be a bird
And send you for a docile child.

On the hill above the town you watch
The weather up and down the valley.
Dear master,
Your children are in danger now
And I, beyond your care,
Am prophet merely of their profound distress.
I have dreamed
That you were dying on the mountain
And spoken to you
In words you would not understand.
The innocence that you are master of
Can only grow more pure by being cold.

My youth was like a clouded crystal
Lighted by disaster from within,
And even now my rage presses utterance on.
Great patient soul,
You do not hear the words, but hear the tears:
Unless you save there is no health in us
Unless you turn the winter down to spring

The birds will not return;
There is no ear but yours in which to say
That love is past all telling strange
And past endurance terrible to feel—
That we can make no use of one another
To solve the sorrow of the thing love is.

This tale for consolation, to a wise man
From a mind that dreams. When once
The flood had withered all the world, and cast
Our seed into a single pod
Which keel made shadows on the mountain tops
Being though warped and rootless
The thronged tree of life,
One messenger returned and sang, "All are desolate,
Held under water like children in a sack,"
A second stopped its beak with a green branch,
But the bird of greatest promise was
A soul that came not back.

THE BAPTIST

Hollow, wavering, imbecile winds
Suspending
Leaves rains wars cries seeds
Over the river ruined by the year
Distract the wild bee mumbling
Golden rod
And all aspiration is bewildered
By the air. The stick I carry
Shatters milkweed pods that yield
Plumed seed to the killed wind
Which turns round also
Flags thrones angers dominations.
Only things immortal are alive.
In the garden
Children quarrel and fall down.
In the graveyard sleep somebody else's people.
I hang like John in the vague air
And tumult of another's destiny.

"BLIND OLD MAN, *take me in your arms and kiss*
my lips. Make me feel how, at the beginning,
you laid her down—beautiful—solitary—on a bed,
in a room and uttered, mouth to mouth, our seed."

✦

"SWEET YOUTH (dilectissime), *go! Punish your pillow!*
When, with a sower's hand—(her shining shovel)—
she scoops up seed and throws it out, the air,
whether windy or still, opens its hysteric

but indifferent arms and takes it in—gift
of a scattering hand. In any case,
some seeds root, if there is light and water.
Therefrom are men (deciduous), and women (evergreen)."

✦

"BLIND OLD MAN, *this is nothing. Kiss my lips.*
And make me see one human face divine.
Light lacks a champion. —Hail, holy light,
the final girlfriend of the western world!"

✦

"SWEET YOUTH (sweetest one), *the payout of a*
long life is second thought. Time to consider
the gifts of the scattering hand, in another light.
What does consideration see by star light

in the hour before the sun? —Sit with me now.
It is the cool, the shadowy hour before dawn.
Among falling leaves, and branches evergreen,
in this quiet air, tell me what you see."

GETTING THE CHILD TO BED

Getting the child to bed is awful work,
Committing that rage to sleep that will not sleep.
The lie rots in my throat saying, "O.K.
There *is* balm in Gilead. Go to bed.
Honey of generation has betrayed us both."
And truly it is no wild surmise of darkness
Nor Pisgah purview of Canaan drowned in blood
But only my child saying its say in bed.

If madness ever covers me, the caul contract
That now but loosely insinuates a shroud
I shall go howling into the conscious grave
(God keep children from the power of the dog)
Follow that note into the uttering horn
Awake in the womb from which I was born.

The hard problem is, what is our interest in
the death of the sun, "this voyage to extinction":
no more past, no more passing, and no more
to come. —The infinite idea of justice.

Hey kid! What song do the sirens sing? On a
solitary rock in the ocean of AWARE
(WAR in it), A and E are the guardians of SAYING.
The trumpets of announcement are I OWE YOU.

The sirens do not know the whole story. But
they do know all the stories. In that difference
(LOVELY GENITAL) we live. The sirens say:
"There is nothing like what happens to each one."

Two boats on a starboard tack round the MARK.
One 100 yards ahead, but a quarter mile
down wind. Both boats head upwind and trim sail.
The boat closest to us carries two jibs

and a spinnaker. The spinnaker halyard
is jammed. That will be fatal. Naked men
(fine looking, seen from below) climb the mast
to free the fouled block. They do not succeed.

The sunlight aloft notes every limb.
Listen, kid. The sirens' song is about
AFFECTIONS, of triumph and taste (strange anagram
of state), lost at sea, on the ocean of AWARE

mind. — *Stiff winds offshore rake the cumbered deck,*
blowing from the right. The MARK is to starboard,
too far to make on this tack as things are,
dilectissima, *or can be.*

With all my awkwardnesses hanging about me like trophies
From Algeciras for the Azores I set out
Under daedalean loneliness of sails;

With trombones from the quays, and streamers rising in the drafts,
Elate and sundered as tears, and with a shout
When the wind rose out of the land,

We towed our loves like rafts into the long tack West.
Mind's word, when it comes, is always departure.
My heart disbelieves the islands.

Priests are always listening; they depart as easily
As God is light; but we who walk
In twos, and lonely even then—

What home out of the alienation of obedience
Can seas throw up to satisfy a man,
Heart stuffed with farewell?

Not absurdity but those I left kept me from rest,
When African and Spanish deserts ranged
Downwind like kites and disappeared.

When from the gates of heaven roll floods of denial
What landfall can recall the still
Waters that restore the soul?

Journey was the wage that built and caulked that boat
Among waterless fields, which then
Was womb to the whole earth.

But of that crew was one climbed down from the black hull
And wrote, even on Ararat, curses
Against the rainbow, being alone.

At the triumphant end of the long fetch of the greatest wave
Age's obscenity is still love's wrong
And grass is seasonally green.

After the stress and blight of great rains to see
Loved faces in a clearer light,
These are the islands of deity.

1955

In my head is a theater. Here
I sit

day and night
summer and winter.

"Come, Creator Spirit, in whatever form."
Everything that CAN appear to me

shows up at one time or another
in this theater.

Spring comes. But also winter.
And then more wintry winter,

masked and veiled.

PART FIVE

blaze

Total eclipse of the sun. Jan. 7 1932.
The cows come home at the wrong time. All the
dogs disappear. The mare foals. Sunlight
slides downward like an unsteerable ship

caught (rudderless) in an inexorable
drift to the left. —Whenever, after that,
I open my eyes, as I do now open
my eyes, or when I reach out to touch you,

or when I sit alone in the mind-room made
quiet by me, eyes closed under each lid,
the same thing happens. Body and soul,
hull and sail, drown. A mirror gapes

and swallows the pictured world. Winged Victory
avoids the bow and signals OBLIVION.
—Why then teach so many? "They were all, all
of them just one: unteachable Beatrice."

Here she comes, a dark tangle of shadows,
to remind me of my duty: that sinister
child (MY MOTHER!) who hangs around after class
to ask why I haven't answered her question.

I think of those who wrote good things of love:
The immense pride, the magnanimity
Of the requital, something given
For the thing received, equal to the thing
Received ("Because of me
You shall not die"), each feature
Given back in another form:
All that was given but not shared
Restored.

I think of those whom I have loved.
A voice says "Cry" and I
"What shall I cry?"
Shall I say, "All flesh is grass
And all its goodness
As the flowers of the field?" These are
Comely
But not generous words.
Cry?
What shall I cry?
What can sweeten the taking of this breath?

Let me not be mad.
Let me enter the great hearts rather
Of the deeply in love,
Breathing with their breath
The immense pride, the magnanimity
Of the requital,
Laying up words against the winter of unremembering
Breathing the breath of those who wrote good things of love
"Because of me you shall not die"

Because of me you shall not die.

WORDS
on Machpelah

It is human to sleep, and human also
To resist sleep, climbing the tower
Concious of an immemorial gesture.
So also it is good to hate the silence
And equally good to seek the stilled heart
Of silence, when only the night-stunned breathing
Of the tenement blurs the dark answer.
And so to be human is to move two ways
Turned toward the beloved most as the dear face
Glimmers at the point of vanishing,
And wisdom is to disavow the illusion
Of repose—not sleep or watching.
                                    It all lies
In doing the action which was foretold,
As the goodness of the magic lies
In the fidelity of the preparation.
So, also, it is in death, whether the death
Of others, our true dying, or our own
Which is real only to those others
Toward whom we have prepared it and for whom
It is an elucidation of what was known
But not well-known, as a language
Is learned but not well-learned. So I prepare
The cave, clearing away the brier from the mouth
And resettling the ancient slates,
The webbed runes on them making clear once more,
And all is ready now to receive you,
As the charm is knitted up which is to you
No more than commonplace enchantment
But to me an astonishment so that I murmur,
"My dear, before this time I knew you not."

✦

Stumbling, making our way as best we can,
Across a broken field with a forked stick
Held in the fashion approved by use
Until the stick turns down and rod divines
The sepulcher of water which crosses the plain,
Like a stealthy animal leaving no spoor
And dives to its sleep under the sod
In a feathered burrow with two entrances,
We seek with the dull organs of limited
Attentiveness which are the eye, the ear, the hand
To make our peace in a strange place,
To discover the older burials of our people
Where spirit rises like a new-tapped well
Of water as if from rock.
                              Nor is there finding
Though the land was bought and paid for
With the scrupulosity of a thievish people
Until the dead assert their definitions
And the landscape is suffused
By the faintly discernible intelligences
Of shepherds who follow with assurance
The wavering trails of goats and even of
The lesser animals, toward the perpetual
Lease and broken field where the first dead
Lie and are not risen.
                              There we meet,
As on the ground foretold but undiscovered
Until the occasion of your death whereof
In honor we embrace, as never in life,
Here underground, while all around the fathers
Confer the immortality of night-accustomed eyes.

                              ✦

The fathers were like animals, experts
At being themselves, finished, beyond advising,
Shedding their abstract seed

Into the cavernous body of the maternal air.
This no underground of thrones, nor
Proud Persepolis of phantom gates
Nor wild rose taken whole into the mind.
This place is limestone where the water walked
To which as to a lair they came and here
Set up their names.

As the mind fades
The meaning of the occasion is asserted
In another language. Old men in their stone
Govern the soul, which in its second season
Opens in the night
And rains of the visible abyss and is made
Fertile by strange wings.

We go not to the multitude
But to the few. The contract was, above all,
A legal document, assuring unto Abraham
A grave. Not foxglove for heartbreak
But a place in which we are no more ourselves.

This to be beautiful to you
Set against all this you know of
So ominous, set against it,
Overcome, might overcome.
This to be beautiful, beautiful,
Never alone enough with God
Never enough among fountains
This be beautiful Spring blue.
Leaf love you for this the while
I am with you and the while after
This earth I am standing on, the
Herons and smaller birds possess.
This to be beautiful to you
The downward fire I spoke of
The eel grass, the snowy path,
The wide shore, the wide shore.
Speak of it, speak it, unceasing, all
These lines to the tomb, O turning tree,
Set against all this you know of
Overcome, will, overcome.
Grave tree of the dark plowland under,
I will will the whole time to you:
Falling water, wave falling, dew
Dust, horses, spirits, Spirit.

THE MURDERER

"O kid! Forget their words! Think for yourself."
Old man! I didn't understand. But now I get it.

— At a great distance, we both heard something.
First you said, "Do you hear that?" And I DID.

Then we both thought the same thought:
The thrush has returned from the waste and void.

Now listen to the new thrush song: "How beautiful!
The numberless crossings of light and shadow at dawn.

How beautiful! That murderous bright stalker, the sun.
Forget his sweet words. O Philosopher,

there is nothing in the world that is like pain.
For that reason, the true poem is not known

and noon is the end of the trueing of song.
When the sun sets, more truth is seen."

"O kid! the thrush has returned from the void."
—Old man! As shadows fall, understanding comes.

Only in a loved face, where life
Time out of mind
Practiced its serenist altitudes
And showings
In gestures of greeting too familiar
To acknowledge
Is death known
As in himself he is.
The face of death is death in a loved face.

The dying mind—
The dying mind, more than another,
Draws near
The element so long loved and refused.
O chaste heart, broken by the stone,
O spirit, spirit, spirit,
How remote your wars!

               Vital it is
Under the world's signs, vital
And more vital, the storm of death.

When I arise from dreams of comforting
And see the snows how they enhance the dawn,
Nothing assuages, no miracle enters in.
The wound bereaves, the wound makes whole.
Blessed is the wound.

THE WRECK

In another part of the empire
 Stormed at sea
My cat boat Deuteronomy
 Was stove and sunk.

The watchman was burying an uncle
 Made fourth on the coffin
While Deuteronomy cracked her sides.
 He should have remembered.

O watchman, good watchman
 Hope hope
The vessel has not taken sand to its very heart.
 We meet again gladly.

THE GHOST

When I shall die, go up into the tower.
The birds below will seem about to fly.
There will be sunlight like a downward fire.

Fools rise from bed to strike the crowned hour.
Death is the loss of one imperfect eye.
When I shall die, go up into the tower.

The heart that flamed fire will at last devour.
The ash be nothing to the ear or eye.
There will be sunlight like a downward fire.

The birds of song will never seem to tire.
The distance will go up like a sweet cry.
When I shall die, go up into the tower.

What I shall be when I am on the pyre
Will not be anything to you or me.
There will be sunlight like a downward fire.

O lady, crowned with this amazing power,
It all depends at last on what you see.
When I shall die, go up into the tower.
There will be sunlight like a downward fire.

SWEET BIRD, SING

Poetry is something
people do
in response to
an obscure demand:
("Sweet bird, sing").

On a day, there arrives
at the swept doorstep, or
appears under a tree,
a complete life
("Sweet bird, sing").

On a day, there arrives
the first sight
of ocean. Mother,
your menstrual wave
("Sweet bird, sing").

On a day, there arrives
(everything arrives)
a big stone.
—Who can lift this thing?
("Sweet bird, sing").

The hammer
in my right hand
strikes it again
and again.
("Sweet bird, sing").

But I swear to you!
My left hand is
still your prophet,
mother Beatrice.
("Sweet bird, sing").

PART SIX

the house sparrow

COME INTO MY GARDEN

Come into my garden. This August is the last.
This night the last summer night.

This hour, the last hour of the night before sunrise.
I think of you, day and night. —Dilectissima,

come into my garden, before the sun. Take my hand
in the dark. "How cold the air."

✦

"How cold you are." The first step down is
a high step. Sublime breath

swells and subsides in the garden among leaves,
each one an emerald sentence

spoken by the oak in the dark. In its mysterious well,
the oak stands sentinel.

✦

Here is a path. It is for considering.
Look left. Consider, in this dark:

"Tiger Lily."
Look right. Consider:

"Bleeding Heart."
Listen. Someone comes.

✦

It is parent
dawn.

She: "Look at the path!" He: "What do you see?"
She: "The path is strewn with letters."

"Dilectissima, *out of these letters I can form no word.*"
Allen, *out of these letters no word can be formed.*

I came upon the order of my life
One evening in a sensual mood
While reading in an ancient author
I have never understood.
I came upon the order of my life
As one would meet a madman with a knife
In a familar but strangely darkened wood.
Surely to be worthy is to KNOW. . .
More dignified, or more bizarre,
Leaving me more changed?

In late July, when all the early flowers
Were quite spent and Spring with its joy was gone,
The day grew cloudy toward the afternoon.
At last we could not say the sun had set
Or that it had not. Without sight of the sky
We speculated on the time of day
Like perpetual workers underground
Or like the learned, or blind, or like two lovers.
I said, being the man I was,
"Lest the gorgeous sunset be forgot
I will presume to rise above the clouds
And see the sun go down," and yet I could not,
Being the man I was, and was ashamed.
You said, "It is now twilight. Soon it will
Be night. We are walking slowly home.
It makes no difference about the time of day."
And still I asked, "What time is it?
Without sunset, without star-rise I cease
to be a man. . . ." Indeed, I was quite absurd.
Lost in a familiar field at twilight,
Dizzy from staring at the overcast
Sky of my life and time, I would have
Stopped right there and died had I the strength.
But you without a thought had led me home.

This, then, is the end of speculation—
This certainty about the way you go.
Night and day, loved or unloved. The darkened sky
Brings rain, rain yields to starlight,
Stars to the somewhat misty morning,
And clear day clouding toward the afternoon.
These things like loving have no place in time.
The road runs through them, for it can't go round.

God is a person
who announces
the principle
of his continuing
existence
in the form
of rules.
He is close
to hand
but hard
to grasp
(as the poet says)
like this house
sparrow
warbling on
my ledge
the other side
of glass.
Suddenly
since April
I am aware
of birdsong.
What is the rule
announced by god
at the beginning
of time
for the sparrow
at my window?
"Let everything
the sparrow sings
be true.
June again
June again
blue."

So, when at last
the June is flown
and storms begin,
the house sparrow
must warble on.
And then
be silent for a time.
After that gone.

AMESBURY

Of the villages I remember the streams
Of the streams weed-walking water birds
Fly-catching in the cold rain and water-lilies
Filling like doomed ships. Under water
Something tangles and untangles. I am
None of this. What's Guinevere to Jews?
Someone they would not think of for themselves.

Antediluvian, the downs, the chalk,
The flints they made the church and abbey of.
And how did flints get here? The explanations
Make no sense. The poppies in that rotted
Wall are not *my* allegories of love
And sleep. This is somebody else's mind;
For me, madness. I make my way. The rain

Dissolves the map, the road. I am not Saul
To fall down and come up another man.
This stream is not a stream, but water
In a clovered field knowing its way.
Tourist, not traveler, I see the sights
At Amesbury where Guinevere, they say,
Stopped loving and combed out her hair.

Stonehenge, by the wet road three miles,
Is not in Malory. He could ignore it.
I have no serious persuasion
To distract the mind. I see what's here—
Like a philosopher. O Lady Guinevere,
Fallen among thieves, we do receive but what
We give and in our life alone we live.

Who dragged these monuments to Sarum
Sweating the cold covenant of a dark
Rainbow after rain? Terror is among
The vicious elements that open
The frontiers. I feel myself akin to
That elder inhabitant, the ones who made
Stone circles under uncovenanted stars.

The rain persists. Nothing ever happens.
Nothing except the keeping down of lust,
That idle fisherman at Grendel's mere,
Heat without light, light without a way,
Or with a way invisible, but from the air
Making soft ridges in the ripening corn
Which serve age after age to break the plow.

A TREE OF TWO SEASONS

1

What does not express itself is evil
An armored thing
A reasonless blow, an unseasonable wind—
Whatever it is, let it declare itself
Not, as now, be known by rages, wounds
Elations. crowds, winters, cries.
Let it be manifest. The mind alone
Is nothing, a garden outside of nature.

2

Seeing is your most blessed way.
It is an angel of all that is
For which some preparation must be made,
Some suffering of sleep to clear the eyes,
An end to which it comes nightly.
Let there be a manner of devout farewell,
A serious and familiar valediction
Of the other parent,
A blessing of the eyes before they close,
A solemn numbering of the winds.

3

When the sun rises in a dark cloud
Flickering with lightning
And night not yet over the horizon behind your back
Takes with it insight of the stars
And space opens outward like a cabinet
Of much secrecy,
Then count the consciousness of all this

The only thing that is—
Imagine the multitude of all the eyes.

4

How seamless is the make of things,
How patient of gaze, how private. Of knowing
Let it be acknowledged the portents are clear
Of indifferent success. All is apparition,
An unconquerable empire,
A tree of two seasons, ever-uttering hero
Of the abyssal winds, planted in time
To blossom in eternity.

5

Waiting for the moment
When the sea has gates, pray that a moment
Be spared you when the mind is clear
For there is no consideration at the instant of death,
So fleeting it may be counted the slightest
Deepening of life's solitude
Or putting from the face of veils
That hide a fading glory.

When the domestic animal becomes *sauvage*
Gives up its cushion and adopts a bed
of rotted leaves behind the shed, when the cat
Strays and the garish bird loses its way in the garden
Leaving the mistress of the house with dreams
And all things go the way they came and are
Busy about their own undoing,

Something enters the garden I do not know
And gives no evidence that it is there
Unless it be the visionary way
The eye despite the shadows apprehends
The ghostly limit of the familiar
And does not stop where the path has always ended
But lingers beyond that, someway on.

Then begins the song of the chickadee,
Sucking and blowing on its instrument,
Like someone singing with a deep intent
To something standing very much apart,
Not caring if whatever hears is kind
Undoing all the purposes of mind
Making the garden larger than before.

Walking by the lake to find out love
I met a man in black. The waves ran high,
Although there was no wind. The dawn was due
And overdue.
The land's rage spent itself in dream.
He stood there (on a skull painted
By someone to warn swimmers of rocks),
Not close to me, but close enough
So I heard him when he said,
"There's something in the waves out there."
I said, "It is the rocks," and turned away
Toward where the waves flamed white.
He was a strange man.
I thought we never could have touched.
But, then, from the wild tumult came a stroke of light
And up upon the lakeshore near Chicago
Six wild horses drew the chariot of the sun.

And now, in sleep, there comes this memory of triumph
Compelling me to yell, "O rock, rock, rock,"
Standing above me like a great wind
And forcing out laughter shout after shout
"Is it I, is it I who am wracked with joy
Who say Yes, Yes, Yes?"
Until my voice is not my voice
But old, forgotten phantom voices
Torn with exultation.

       —There comes to me in sleep
A shout of triumph, setting myself against myself,
Whipping me with cords until I dance
Bruising my body with its own lost violence
Waking me,
   astounded by the lark and terror of the morning.

POMPEII

My rage is more than I can bear in silence.
I died once in Pompeii in a gilded bath
Wearing the belt of my servitude. Dense,
Dry ash covered my sex and ended my wrath.

Now when the craters of the Spring pour out a path
Of seed upon the infertile air, my sense
Of things is changed, and my forgotten breath
Is an oppression, my rage is so intense.

I and my friends do not seek liberation
That comes from any kind of knowing.
We insist that we are of nature, and nothing
The Spring blesses is alien from us. The sea
Is in our hearts, and the austerity of the gull's wing
Chastens, uplifts us, and is invitation.

This incomplete life ends
the same as a complete life.
There is no difference.
You are the figure of all figures
but it is no help. It makes
no difference to you.
Better there be no East,
the sun rises in any case,
or West,
and sets
over your leafy suburb.
Felicitous speaking
makes no difference.
There is nothing in it
for another one
whether it happens
or does not
that "suddenly I see your face."

PART SEVEN

among the dead at troy

Among the dead at Troy
above
and among the
dead men
there,
shadows of a scattering
hand.

God kills and makes
alive.
There can be no harm
that the sounds
of
our speaking
die away

and are lost
—because God is begotten
(not made)
whenever we greet
one another
and are known
one to the other

and find our way.
In the name
of man and woman
let there be
poetless
song.
Light is

poetless song,
honors the body

of each man and woman,
towers of the unowned word.
Our body
is the seamark to all the mariners,
the high and the

far seen
house.
As for the rages,
as for the wars, the years,
pity us who pass,
O all you who pass.
State, property, religion

those are the treasonous
those are the sacrilege.
Pity us
as for the towers,
one at a time
and all together:
the greatest wrong,

the highest song.
Pity us,
I beg you
and sing the unmade,
the begotten only.
Sing the poetless song.
There is no harm

if it is scattered.

MOVING THE TREES AROUND
(chant poem with a refrain)

1. What is the sound in the shell of the sea?
   What rumbles in the ground?
   Rockefeller and Kublai Khan are moving the trees around.

Moving the trees around, my friend, moving the trees around.
Rockefeller and Kublai Khan are moving the trees around.

2. It isn't the sea you hear in the shell
   And it isn't the blood going round
   It's Rockefeller and Kublai Khan moving trees around.

Moving the trees around, my friend, moving the trees around.
Rockefeller and Kublai Khan are moving the trees around.

3. It's a thing the great do in their later years,
   The eyes gone dim but the will still sound,
   Rockefeller and Kublai Khan start moving trees around.

Moving the trees, etc.

4. In their later years they grow restless and strange,
   Having buried their children, forgotten their jokes,
   Rockefeller and Kublai Khan take it out on the oaks.

Moving the trees, etc.

5. It isn't anxiety calling the tune
   And it sure as Hell's not Jesus Christ
   It's Rockefeller and Kublai Kahn with a shadowy tree in each
   fist.

Moving the trees, etc.

6. What are the shapes that darken the hill?
   What comes from the sea with a roar?
   It's Rockefeller and Kublai Khan planting forests of war.

Moving the trees, etc.

7. It isn't any beast of the Lord
   Nor another shape of pain.
   It's Rockefeller and Kublai Khan out in wind and rain.

Moving the trees, etc.

8. The old men, restless and weeping a bit,
   Are planting their gardens both Spring and Fall.
   But you and I, though we live to be old, will never enjoy them at all.

Moving the trees, etc.

9. They do it because they *like* the work.
   It's their idea of fun.
   And the trees they are planting are brighter by far than the moon
                                                    and the sun.

Moving the trees, etc.

10. O what gouty Captains with death in their eyes
    Are building Eden again?
    It's Rockefeller and Kublai Khan, the heart and the brain.

Moving the trees, etc.

11. What is the light that bewilders the eye?
    What sound as of laboring cars?
    The tree of life that was shaken and dry is moving among the stars.

Moving the trees around, my friend, moving the trees around.
Rockefeller and Kublai Khan are moving the trees around.

EVERYWHERE I FIND THE JEWS KILLING THE IMAGINATION

Everywhere I find the Jews killing the imagination
Inventing death, enshrining the void in shrines
And the names of things in hard rock
Nailing the hawk to the barn door of the Law
Suppressing the understanding of words
Binding the colors of daylight.

Everywhere I find the Jews killing the imagination
Which will not let them die,
Which sent unblessed Mormon O'Grady to Salt Lake in 1868,
Unnumbered avatar of Ahasuerus—
Keeping the world by dark conspiratorial suspensions of disbelief,
Weird hunters of the phantom dragon by which they live.

For the Jew has the key or combination or whatever
Of the Seventh Seal (Milton knew the first three numbers)
Which will return the Jew alone
By way of the six-winged vulva of the God-Mother
To Eden, drawing all things with him ("clouds of glory").
And everywhere I find the Jews killing the imagination which is love,

Melting the golden calf into gleaming gigantic dead grape clusters,
Sleeping in the face of the sun,
Nailing down the coffin-lid on the still-breathing son of God,
Killing the imagination even in the streets of Jerusalem.
The Jew lives by killing.
The clothes of the condemned are the perquisites of the executioner,

Whose Lord is a rock, at whose heart the phantom dead
Crouch in the dark like fossil spoors.
But when the Jew is gone, O sons of man, when the Jew is gone
And the lilies of the field erupt through the macadam of the New
                                                    Jerusalem

When the Jew has been swallowed up by the great swallower
Who utters the *logos* he cannot spell,

When the last Jew is finally hunted down in St. Louis,
When the Jew is gone, O meek inheritors,
And the lion and the lamb lie down together—at last
And there is no more sea and no more seafaring
When the last Jew has bedded down in the bosom of Abraham
And forgot the name of his God

Then the imagination will rise up like a bad cloud
The veil rent, the sun put out, and the great stone rolled away
Like a blown weed,
And we shall all begin to scream without waking to Papa
Battering a squirrel with a bloody shoetree behind a dead radiator
In the nightmare dream of settling permanently in America.

Like Spring, but with a low sun. What season?
Green hairs on the hills, but the time is wrong.
Emptiness I can breathe, not air. The time
Declares, "He is not in me." *But he is here.*

If he is here, why is the season wrong,
This light so low, and air unsheltering,
The time wrecked, the fierce stream fallen down,
The low sun hot, the snow lying along?

"Who am so skillful with you, you do not know.
Lie down. You are not beautiful. But I am strong.
The known times did you no good at all.
The night is full of flares. The night is day.
Open your mouth. I love you. You do not know.
In a low sun unsheltering great rains fall."

I grow boat-wings
oars, sails.

Sail simplifies but does
not cure.

Wreck is the fact.
Sail

is the sower's cast, the wheat in shovels
thrown out

over the threshing floor,
ocean.

The winds sort living
and dead.

Winds of time,
winds of war

sort seed.
Some

reach
the living.

Some
die away

and the cries begin.
I heard you

for the first time at sea,
like the swell.

Now we pass, you and me,
under the lighthouse

and sighing cape and tower
isle, Patmos.

Patmos
We see.

Cold spring of Bandusia, brighter than glass,
Blood must be devoted
(Wine and flowers are
Almost images already)
To you
Nerveless, deep,

In whom the weary animal surprises
The face of hope,
In whom August with her whips and passions
Cannot find the imaged flock

Coldest fountain, among fountains of note,
Fountain of the cave
Fountain of the cave and oak.

AS FOR THE TOWERS
(unison chant)

As for the towers, the apple forests
As for the towers, the great steeple
As for the towers, the dark peaks

As for the towers, the glassy oceans
As for the towers, words whiten
As for the towers, all is still

All is still, as for the towers
Birds brighten, as for the towers
Death is weary, as for the towers

He did not come, as for the towers
The apple forests, the great steeples
The glassy oceans, the dark peaks

The snows, the children, as for the towers
Words whiten, as for the towers
As for the towers, all is still.

✦

As for the towers, there is a banner
As for the towers, there is a music
As for the towers, there is a rage

There is a rage, as for the towers
There is a winter, as for the towers
The glassy oceans, the dark peaks

The snow, the children, as for the towers
Bells and echoes, as for the towers
As for the towers, all is still

Then be loving, as for the towers
Then be secret, as for the towers
Then be true, as for the towers.

✦

As for the towers, voices sharpen
As for the towers, voices answer
As for the towers, voices burn

As for the towers, skies are yellow
As for the towers, sleep is broken
As for the towers, the sun is slow

As for the towers, as for the towers
As for the towers, as for the towers
As for the towers, as for the towers

I lay me down, as for the towers
I lay me down, I lay me down
The apple forests, the glassy oceans

The snows, the children, as for the towers
And the crowns, as for the towers
The flaming crowns, as for the towers.

✦

As for the towers, O long awaited
As for the towers, as for the towers
As for the towers, as for the towers

And the shadows, as for the towers
Larks and spirits, as for the towers
Labor and pain, as for the towers

Sorrow and death, as for the towers
He will not come, as for the towers
As for the towers, as for the towers

Do not forget, as for the towers
Love and work, as for the towers
Wake and sleep, as for the towers

As for the towers, as for the towers
Boats at evening, as for the towers
Boats at evening, as for the towers.

✦

Winds widen, as for the towers
Stars stare, as for the towers
All is still, as for the towers

Is there an end, as for the towers
Is there an end, as for the towers
Is there an end, as for the towers

When the webs, as for the towers
When the larks, as for the towers
When the years, as for the towers

As for the towers, as for the towers
And the wars, as for the towers
And the sweats, as for the towers

And the graves that overshadow, as for the towers
And the graves that overshadow, as for the towers
As for the towers, as for the towers.

✦

He did not come, as for the towers
He did not come, as for the towers
O long awaited, as for the towers

The rocks and rivers, as for the towers
Webs and winds, as for the towers
Rage and music, as for the towers

Then be loving, as for the towers
Then be secret, as for the towers
Then be true, as for the towers

As for the towers, as for the towers
Birds brighten, as for the towers
As for the towers, all is still

Boats at evening, as for the towers
O long awaited, as for the towers
As for the towers, as for the towers.

✦

I am with you, as for the towers
I am with you, as for the towers
I am with you, as for the towers

And the banners, as for the towers
And the spirits, as for the towers
And the larks, as for the towers

And the webs, as for the towers
And the rage, as for the towers
And the years, as for the towers

Bells and echoes, as for the towers
The apple forests, the great steeples
The glassy oceans, the dark peaks

The snows, the children, as for the towers
As for the towers, I am with you
I am with you, all is still.

✦

It is finished, as for the towers
The bells and echoes, as for the towers
Boats at evening, as for the towers

As for the towers, rage and music
As for the towers, rocks and rivers
As for the towers, webs and winds

Death is weary, as for the towers
Birds brighten, as for the towers
The apple forests, the great steeples

The dark peaks, the glassy oceans
The snows, the children, as for the towers
As for the towers, all is still

Then be loving, as for the towers
Then be secret, as for the towers
Then be true, as for the towers
As for the towers, as for the towers.

O kid! I didn't understand. But now I get it.
Forget their words! Look around for yourself.

At a great distance, we heard something. First
you said, "Do you hear that?" And I DID hear it.

Then we both thought the same thought:
The thrush has returned from the waste and void.

✦

I didn't understand. But, then, I did understand.
Listen to the thrush returned from the waste:

"Every death destroys the final philosopher.
In a numbered year, among numberless crossings

of light and shadow, at dawn, the shadows are
in peril, from the bright stalker—the sun.

✦

Forget his sweet words. If there is to be any
truthful poem, then it will not be understandable

for the very reason that it is true."
"But why must that be so. . . ?"

"Because there MAY be something in the world
that is like joy, as Dante says there is,

✦

BUT there is nothing in the world that is like pain.
For that reason, the true poem is not known

and noon is the end of the trueing of song.
As the sun sets, more truth is seen.

The final philosopher writes 'subject.' THEN 'object.'
As the shadows fall, so understanding comes."